Leaders

Unleashed

Leading Without Anxiety

To my family
and all leaders everywhere

Leadership Unleashed

Leading Without Anxiety

Jessie Upp, M.S.

Epoch Media
Seattle, Washington

Cover Image by Ruff Wear, Knot-a-Leash™
Internal Design by Jessie Upp
Author photograph by Karin Bigelow

This publication is designed to provide authoritative information in regard to the subject matter covered. It is sold with the understanding that the publisher is not engaged in rendering legal, accounting, or other professional service. If legal advice or other expert assistance is required, the services of a competent or professional person should be sought. – *From A Declaration of Principles Jointed Adopted by a Committee of the American Bar Association and a Committee of Publishers and Associations.*

All brand names and product names used in this book are trademarks of their respective holders. Epoch Media is not associated with any product or vendor in this book. Epoch Media books may be purchased for educational or business use.

FIRST EDITION

All inquires should be addressed to:
Epoch Media
PO Box 84
Marblemount, WA 98267

Library of Congress Cataloging-in-Publication Data is available upon request.

International Standard Book No.: 978-0-615-36888-7

Printed and bound in the United States of America.
10 9 8 7 6 5 4 3 2 1

Leading Without Anxiety

Leadership is about following concepts.

J.R.R. Tolkien said it eloquently: "It does not do to leave a live dragon out of your calculations, if you live near him." I think Tolkien meant that if I close my eyes to ignore the hole in front of me, it might not be an effective strategy while walking. It means "Pay attention to all the stuff." It means I should know where my anxieties are. They might lie where the dragon lives...in my anxieties that arrive with my concepts, or thoughts.

It occurs to me that, as a leader, I am only motivated by the concepts I am following. In this way, I see leaders and followers as the same, both adhering to certain thoughts. Have you ever noticed how we react to our own imaginations and not to people? It takes an empowered imagination to lead others and I've spent most of my life exploring this topic of metacognition. In this exploration, I've come to realize that leadership is not about absolutes, control, manipulation, management, or power. It's about effective influence.

If we are anxious, chances are that followers will be anxious as well. More importantly note, followers may not want to pursue such influence at all. It doesn't matter if it's an employee, a family member, a friend or a community. They follow people that ignite self-empowering traits. One of the most powerful attributes of mankind is projection. We can easily project thoughts onto everything and everyone we experience. This can apply to everything, from sentences to the concept of love. For instance, I see:

- o I don't finish other people's sentences. I finish my own.
- o How terrible listeners are listening to their own thoughts, just as good listeners also listen to their own thoughts.
- o Nobody judges me. They are simply judging their own thoughts.
- o The way someone looks at me reflects back to me what I think of me.
- o When I fall in love with someone, I am simply falling in love with myself all over again.
- o The most natural thing that can happen is that I don't get what I'm hoping for.
- o Thoughts just land on me and I call them my own.
- o I don't control my thoughts and that leaves me wondering who is really leading.

ATTEMPTING TO LEAD

Every one of us has tried to influence people with techniques we've learned from others. Many of us continue to use specific techniques that don't lead, such as getting angry or withdrawing. These techniques don't help us get what we want. They don't allow the successful transfer of ideas. They keep us leashed to our own concepts as they attempt to leash others. Our anxieties lead many us and we follow. We become followers to concepts that help us fall into a gigantic hole we were trying to build a bridge over.

So, why do we keep pursuing these concepts? Why do we keep attempting to lead this way? It must provide some sort of outlet to release anxieties. Still, what if we didn't have these anxieties to try to release in the first place?

I have learned that I don't HAVE to follow any thought. I can see it land on me and either respectfully hold it, or flick it off like a beetle.

TO LEASH OR UNLEASH?

You may want to know your dragons and the motivating sources of your anxieties. Doing so will result in effective leadership and influence.

I make plans, but sometimes I get caught up in this plan that I don't notice what is available in the present - the most integral part of any vision.

In this book, you may find one or more concepts you have been following. They either derive from a mentality of "not having" or "having". The "not having" thoughts show up with anxiety, coupled with complaining, unhealthy habits, avoidance, exhaustion, and even illness.

The thoughts anchored in "having" kick my anxious thoughts to the curb. Now I have the choice to use this tool and lead without anxiety.

The most effective leaders realize anxiety derives from unavailable *(have not)* concepts. These leaders choose to pay attention to what is presently available *(have concepts)* to fluidly and graciously move to the next experience.

We all know how to lead with anxiety. Do you know how to lead without it? Do you know how to be anxious-free, even when the circumstances don't warrant it?

About This Book

This book isn't about learning to persuade others. **Leadership Unleashed** is about exploring ways to drop the leash of control - the illusion of control. It's about exuding leadership principles that keep us on our tracks. Even though anxiety can be construed in a positive light, anxiety can derail us, too.

These are 100 observations that aren't ultimate truths. Each simply serves as different viewpoints that **free me from anxiety**. Since many observations are paradoxical, I continue to refine my interpretations. Therefore, in this book version, I leave the interpretations up to you. It is a journey for all of us.

Anxiousness entails worry, nervousness, uneasiness, restlessness and fear of not getting what we want or losing what we already have. Even though anxiety can serve us when it comes to physical safety, it often takes the main stage when it comes to conceptual safety. This is very limiting. If anxiety is the main motivator for attempting leadership, we ourselves, are limited. So, I define anxiety as a deterrent to effective leadership. Anxiety focuses our attention on what we didn't get and this deters us from focusing on what we do have in order to lead ourselves into our next experience.

After you are free from anxiety, you can lead in an entirely new way, while the concepts of punishment, manipulation and authority find their equal.

Buying into the uncertainty principle*, it's not that I have "figured out" the age old paradox of time/observation. That being that time moves forward, or that we all share different experiences. I'm simply illuminated by different perspectives. For example, I'm illuminated to view time as standing still, as a series of still pictures contained in a movie. I'm also illuminated by the viewpoint that we all share the same experience (seeking happiness).

* Uncertainty Principle – That is, the more precisely one property is known, the less precisely the other can be known.

Interpretations

On purchasing this book, interpretations in all forms (textual, visual, audio, video) are accessible on the website at www.JessieUpp.com. These include both the interpretations of Jessie Upp and the readers of this book, like you.

VISUAL: You are invited to draw your stick-figure interpretations of each observation in each box. There, you can draw out the way you "see" the world in a way that doesn't happen while thinking, or writing.

TEXTUAL: Each subsequent page is left blank for word-brain interpretations and further questions. **For each observation, you are invited to ask yourself, "As a leader, how could this open up something new for me?"**

VIDEO: As with visual or textual, you are welcome to share your audio/video interpretations at the learning community at www.JessieUpp.com.

Leashed Concepts: # 1-64

Leashed concepts derive from the mentality of "not having", or as a leash of control. Following these concepts often creates anxiety. It is rare to effectively lead others using these techniques when they are over-valued. They often stimulate anxiety in others, rather than inspiring an empowered following.

Unleashed Concepts: # 65-100

Unleashed concepts derive from the mentality of "having" - paying attention to what is available. The most effective leaders stay calm, cool and collected. They unleash their potential!

This is not a book for enticing agreement or disagreement. From leading in the family home to the corporate board room, your answers will entice you in your own experience. Maybe you will be compelled to negate the observation, or disprove it. Even in that case, opportunity awaits you.

Metaphorically speaking, it is an invitation to walk to the other side of the room and see your thoughts from a different angle. In all angles and viewpoints, I see a possible truth...sitting perfectly. In this possible truth, your answer allows you to move to another position where even more questions are born. Perhaps your answers will act as an opening, helping to awaken dormant empathy, or even a grand new insight.

— 1 —

Feeling Anxious about a Concept

Illustrate Here

If anxiety motivates me, I will lead anxiously.

— 2 —

Projecting a Concept

I am continually reinforced for thinking you are not me, even though I create everything about you.

My Interpretations

For each observation, challenge yourself to find an angle of truth, rather than agreeing/disagreeing with "a" truth.

Ample space is left for musing notes, questions or your own observations. Take this example below:

Hmm...I feel like I want to argue with Epigram #2, but I know that my intent is to simply see an angle of truth...

I do understand how I interpret everything I hear or see. In this interpretation, I create everything I notice. In essence, everything I notice is me.

This brings me a profound sense of freedom as I don't have to take time to manipulate others to seeing me a certain way any more!

— 3 —

Reminiscing About a Concept

*When I have anxious thoughts,
I'm experiencing a loss from the past.*

— 4 —

Opposing a Concept

*If I oppose what already happened,
I can't lead right now.*

My Interpretations

_____

_____

_____

_____

_____

_____

_____

_____

_____

_____

_____

_____

_____

_____

_____

− 5 −

Offended by a Concept

No one can offend me. I only offend myself.

− 6 −

Rejected by a Concept

I don't argue with someone else's decision.
I argue with my own rejection.

My Interpretations

_____

_____

_____

_____

_____

_____

_____

_____

_____

_____

_____

_____

_____

_____

− 7 −

Excessive Concerns About a Concept

*Excessive concerns about being **Right**
will lead me right to the exact place
I spend so much time avoiding.*

− 8 −

Complaining About a Concept

When I complain, I am a victim.

My Interpretations

_____

_____

_____

_____

_____

_____

_____

_____

_____

_____

_____

_____

_____

_____

_____

– 9 –
Trying to Fulfill a Concept

I'm observing how we're all just trying different methods to be noticed.

– 10 –
Seeking Praise of a Concept

When I want praise and I get it, they are only praising their own thoughts.

My Interpretations

_____

_____

_____

_____

_____

_____

_____

_____

_____

_____

_____

_____

_____

_____

_____

_____

_____

— 11 —

Desiring Acknowledgement of a Concept

I tried very hard to make people know me in a certain way, but I never knew if I was really successful.

— 12 —

Hiding Behind a Concept

Trying to make someone see me as another "me" will leave "me" hiding behind me.

My Interpretations

_____

_____

_____

_____

_____

_____

_____

_____

_____

_____

_____

_____

_____

_____

_____

_____

_____

— 13 —

Expecting a Fulfilled a Concept

My expectations often lead me to a destination of putting my happiness on hold.

— 14 —

Projecting a Lost a Concept

The only sources of my anxious mind come from a projected loss in the past or future.

My Interpretations

_____

_____

_____

_____

_____

_____

_____

_____

_____

_____

_____

_____

_____

_____

_____

_____

_____

_____

_____

— 15 —

Avoiding a Concept

Prevention is attempting to avoid a concept I hold.

— 16 —

Addicted to a Concept

I'm not addicted to any vice as much as I am addicted to my concepts.

My Interpretations

_____

_____

_____

_____

_____

_____

_____

_____

_____

_____

_____

_____

_____

_____

_____

− 17 −

Inventing a Concept of Others

When I think about others,
I explore how I am projecting myself onto them.

− 18 −

Missing a Fulfilled Concept

I don't really miss anyone.
I miss who I'm being when I'm around them.

My Interpretations

_____

_____

_____

_____

_____

_____

_____

_____

_____

_____

_____

_____

_____

_____

_____

_____

_____

− 19 −

Not Finished Living Out a Concept

My current negative feelings are an outcome of an event that has already been completed.

− 20 −

Taken Advantage by a Concept

"They took advantage of me" is a hurtful concept being experienced right now.

My Interpretations

_____

_____

_____

_____

_____

_____

_____

_____

_____

_____

_____

_____

_____

_____

_____

— 21 —

Trying to Change a Concept

My bad mood is really just a result of trying to change something I can't.

— 22 —

Frustrated with a Concept

*I don't get frustrated with anyone.
I get frustrated with my own rejection.*

My Interpretations

_____

_____

_____

_____

_____

_____

_____

_____

_____

_____

_____

_____

_____

_____

_____

— 23 —

Labeling a Concept

How can I love my enemies when I call them an ENEMY in the first place?

— 24 —

Intimidated by a Concept

There is no way a "bully" can't be a reflection of my own beliefs. No one can intimidate me.

My Interpretations

_____

_____

_____

_____

_____

_____

_____

_____

_____

_____

_____

_____

_____

_____

− 25 −

Hurt by a Concept

I hurt myself every time
I have thoughts about being hurt.

− 26 −

Trusting a Concept

If I believe a person is untrustworthy, I seem to do
things to deem that person untrustworthy
and then I become untrustworthy.

My Interpretations

_____

_____

_____

_____

_____

_____

_____

_____

_____

_____

_____

_____

_____

_____

_____

— 27 —

Annoyed by a Concept

Annoyance of others is caused by projecting my own meaning on another person's actions.

— 28 —

Trying to Cease a Concept

When I say No, Don't or Stop to another, I'm really just saying No, Don't or Stop to my own thoughts.

My Interpretations

_____

_____

_____

_____

_____

_____

_____

_____

_____

_____

_____

_____

_____

_____

_____

— 29 —

Angered by a Concept

*When I'm angry, it's because
I'm not getting what I want.*

— 30 —

Battling Over Visual Concepts

My arguments are just battles over images.

My Interpretations

_____

_____

_____

_____

_____

_____

_____

_____

_____

_____

_____

_____

_____

_____

_____

− 31 −

Earning a Concept

To me, money is just a concept
waiting to be earned.

− 32 −

Firing a Concept

To me, being fired or divorced is only being fired
or divorced from a concept.

My Interpretations

_____

_____

_____

_____

_____

_____

_____

_____

_____

_____

_____

_____

_____

_____

_____

_____

— 33 —

Name Calling a Concept

*If I call someone a name,
I'm just naming my own thoughts.*

— 34 —

Becoming a Concept

*If I call someone controlling or a jerk,
I am being controlling or a jerk.*

My Interpretations

— 35—

Pushing a Concept

Every time I think I know what someone else should do, I am holding onto a leash.

— 36—

Hating a Concept

If I hate something or someone, I contribute to war.

My Interpretations

_____

_____

_____

_____

_____

_____

_____

_____

_____

_____

_____

_____

_____

_____

_____

_____

− 37 −

Enforcing a Concept

*By understanding my rules for others,
I understand my lies.*

− 38 −

Forcing Apologies Over a Concept

I see a forced sorry as a forced lie.

My Interpretations

_____

_____

_____

_____

_____

_____

_____

_____

_____

_____

_____

_____

_____

_____

_____

_____

– 39 –

Listening to Concepts

People don't listen to people.
They listen to concepts.

– 40 –

Seeking Proof of a Concept

A nod of agreement is not proof of others
understanding me. They understand themselves.

My Interpretations

_____

_____

_____

_____

_____

_____

_____

_____

_____

_____

_____

_____

_____

_____

— 41 —

Self-Blaming a Concept

Man, I *shouldn't* have done that.

Habits are declarative messages being sent to my robotic mind, yet I still take the blame for them.

— 42 —

Restricting a Conceptual Response

Good.

"My habitual questions of "How Is...or How Was Your Day?" or "How Are You?" can be very restrictive inquiries as they elicit one word declarations describing the last 60,000 moments.

My Interpretations

_____

_____

_____

_____

_____

_____

_____

_____

_____

_____

_____

_____

_____

_____

_____

_____

_____

— 43 —

Hoping for a Concept

> *I wish she would say "thank you" for all that I've done for her...*

When I wrote down what I hoped for someone to finally say to me, I realized that was my hallucination of a world where happiness was on hold.

— 44 —

Drinking a Concept

I see we don't have any habit that doesn't unconsciously work for us, including smoking, drinking, eating (or any vice).

My Interpretations

_____

_____

_____

_____

_____

_____

_____

_____

_____

_____

_____

_____

_____

_____

_____

_____

— 45 —

Resisting a Concept

When I yawn, I'm resisting something in my life and I don't consider it being only a sleep issue.

— 46 —

Fearing a Concept

Just because I don't take a chance, doesn't mean I won't get burned.

My Interpretations

_____

_____

_____

_____

_____

_____

_____

_____

_____

_____

_____

_____

_____

_____

_____

_____

— 47 —

Not Loving a Concept

If I do something I don't love,
I'm not considering all my options.

— 48 —

Attempting to Physically Force a Concept

When I feel the need to physically hurt someone,
I'm trying to teach someone what I'm trying to
learn myself, but haven't.

My Interpretations

— 49 —

Comparing Concepts

When I compare someone else to me, all I'm doing is comparing one part of myself to another (since I've created both comparisons).

— 50 —

Labeling a Concept

I don't see anyone as a good or bad person. They just do good or bad things and THAT is even arguable.

My Interpretations

— 51 —

Projecting a Concept

Most of my exhaustion is a result of seeking peace.

— 52 —

Wanting a Concept Confirmed

A love for doing something changes when I'm doing it for someone else to witness.

My Interpretations

_____

_____

_____

_____

_____

_____

_____

_____

_____

_____

_____

_____

_____

_____

_____

_____

— 53 —

Seeking Respect of a Concept

Nobody can love or respect me as ME...
All they know is their own experience of who I am.

— 54 —

Seeking Completion in a Concept

People don't complete me.
They simply represent my own desirable traits,
already available to and in me.

My Interpretations

_____
_____
_____
_____
_____
_____
_____
_____
_____
_____
_____
_____
_____
_____
_____
_____

— 55—

Bored by a Concept

*If I declare myself as Bored,
I'm just being Boring.*

— 56—

Unorganized Concepts

*A messy space is just a bunch of concepts
yet to be organized.*

My Interpretations

_____

_____

_____

_____

_____

_____

_____

_____

_____

_____

_____

_____

_____

_____

_____

_____

— 57 —

Embarrassed by a Concept

What are they thinking about ME?!?!

If I'm shy, or embarrassed,
I'm leading with selfishness.

— 58 —

Confused by a Concept

People don't confuse me. I confuse myself when
comparing their concepts to mine.

My Interpretations

_____

_____

_____

_____

_____

_____

_____

_____

_____

_____

_____

_____

_____

_____

_____

_____

— 59 —

Not Imagining a Concept

The precursor to saying "can't" is not attempting to imagine another concept.

— 60 —

Impatient with a Concept

Impatience pays attention to what isn't available which doesn't help speed anything up.

My Interpretations

_____

_____

_____

_____

_____

_____

_____

_____

_____

_____

_____

_____

_____

_____

_____

_____

– 61 –

Worried About a Concept

My worry for others give me a fictitious identity of one who is in control.

– 62 –

Trying to Change Another's Concept

To think I can change someone leaves me confirming my own illusion.

My Interpretations

_____

_____

_____

_____

_____

_____

_____

_____

_____

_____

_____

_____

_____

_____

_____

_____

— 63 —

Punishing a Concept

I now see how I can't punish anyone without making it about myself.

— 64 —

Believing a Concept

My deepest held beliefs create my highest levels of anxiety.

My Interpretations

_____

_____

_____

_____

_____

_____

_____

_____

_____

_____

_____

_____

_____

_____

_____

Unleashed Concepts   65–100

The following concepts derive from the mentality of "having", or paying attention to what is available. Leaders motivated by available concepts unleash their potential...

— 65 —

Secured by a Concept

I get secure in the certainty that I create you.

— 66 —

Looking Closely at a Concept

I get motivated when I feel annoyed because I know it's nothing about others. Big or small, annoyances always lead back to me.

My Interpretations

_____

_____

_____

_____

_____

_____

_____

_____

_____

_____

_____

_____

_____

_____

– 67 –

Eavesdropping on My Concepts

As a leader, I cultivate the ability to eavesdrop on my mental conversations.

– 68 –

Taking Responsibility for My Concepts

When I substitute "you" with "I", change becomes my responsibility.

My Interpretations

_____
_____
_____
_____
_____
_____
_____
_____
_____
_____
_____
_____
_____
_____
_____

– 69 –

Disappointed by a Concept

Disappointment is the most profound thing that has led to my self-realization.

– 70 –

Not Believing a Concept

When I stopped believing my thoughts as true, life became even more peaceful to me.

My Interpretations

_____

_____

_____

_____

_____

_____

_____

_____

_____

_____

_____

_____

_____

_____

_____

_____

— 71 —

Finding Love in Any Concept

To me, anger is love disguised.

— 72 —

Available to All Concepts

Once I looked at love as having nothing to do with another, I was finally available to everyone.

My Interpretations

— 73 —

Seeking No Reasons for a Concept

I can't think of any anxious-free reason to believe my anxious thought.

— 74 —

Relating to All Concepts

My relationship with myself is all I have and this is why I only do what I love to do.

My Interpretations

_____

_____

_____

_____

_____

_____

_____

_____

_____

_____

_____

_____

_____

_____

_____

_____

_____

— 75 —

Turning Around Concepts

*I see now that I've been pretending
to listen to someone else
when all I hear are my own interpretations.*

— 76 —

Unfolding Concepts

*Asking myself, "What does that mean?" uncovers
the false belief causing my anxiety.*

My Interpretations

_____

_____

_____

_____

_____

_____

_____

_____

_____

_____

_____

_____

_____

_____

– 77 –

Reminded by a Concept

If I make a rule for others and they don't respond
to it, it's a gentle reminder that
I don't have control over them.

– 78 –

Deciding on Concepts

I've come to understand that people will have
already made decisions about me –
before they even met me.

My Interpretations

_____

_____

_____

_____

_____

_____

_____

_____

_____

_____

_____

_____

_____

_____

_____

_____

_____

_____

– 79 –
Liking, Loving or Hating Concepts

To like, love or hate someone is simply a concept being experienced at a feeling level.

– 80 –
Aware of Self-Conceptualization

My relationships are no longer based on fulfilling each other's imagination, but stimulating each other's imagination.

My Interpretations

_____

_____

_____

_____

_____

_____

_____

_____

_____

_____

_____

_____

_____

_____

— 81 —

Guessing Concepts

If someone asks me why I did what I did, I can only guess by listening to the closest concept that is available to me at that moment.

— 82 —

Pleasured by a Concept

Pleasure is a fulfilled concept.

My Interpretations

_____

_____

_____

_____

_____

_____

_____

_____

_____

_____

_____

_____

_____

_____

_____

_____

_____

Creating Conditions for Concepts

All habits come from the unconscious and that is why I rarely call the shots. I can only create the conditions for my shots to change.

Losing or Gaining a Concept

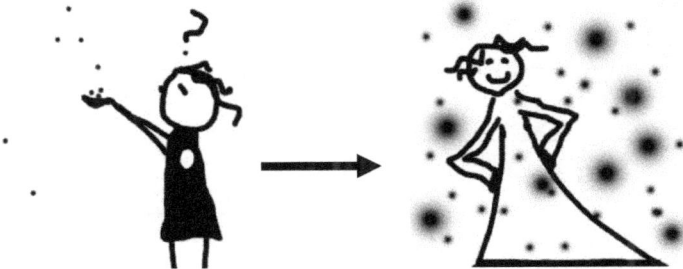

After asking, "Is this it?" about my life, I projected a world of having everything to lose or gain to the world of having nothing to lose or gain.

My Interpretations

— 85 —

Not Counting On Concepts

*I plan on my plans changing so much that
I'm surprised when they actually work out!*

— 86 —

Opening Up to Other Concepts

*A preference is just one of many ways to the same
place. So when I get anxious,
I quickly explore a different preference.*

My Interpretations

— 87 —

Experiencing Shared Concepts

I can see how we ALL may very well be experiencing the same thing.

— 88 —

Not Defending Concepts

You're a Ljuen!

I can't defend anything I don't believe to be true.

My Interpretations

– 89 –

Self-Fulfilled by Concepts

I finally see that no one wants me and this is a very good thing. As others just want to fulfill their imaginations, I can freely fulfill mine.

– 90 –

Acknowledging Self-Induced Concepts

I can't fulfill anyone that doesn't already have the ability to fulfill themselves.

My Interpretations

_____

_____

_____

_____

_____

_____

_____

_____

_____

_____

_____

_____

_____

_____

_____

_____

— 91 —

Learning Concepts

The one learning is teaching.
The one talking is learning.

— 92 —

Experiencing Truths in All Concepts

I'm being a teacher when I'm
not inclined to argue with what I see or hear.

My Interpretations

_____

_____

_____

_____

_____

_____

_____

_____

_____

_____

_____

_____

_____

_____

_____

_____

Smiling at a Concept

*When I light up my face,
it is my ultimate advice for others.*

Discovering Options Through Concepts

Anger
My
Funny
Thoughts
My Parent
Stupid
Enemy
Good
Silk
Respect Work
Vanilla Rock Music
All Children
Love

*If I look at anything as God disguised, it opens
up new learning options for me in the moment.*

My Interpretations

_____

_____

_____

_____

_____

_____

_____

_____

_____

_____

_____

_____

_____

_____

_____

_____

_____

– 95 –

Leading Myself into Concepts

If I am leading others, then I have followers and they are just following their own concepts. So who am I left leading? Myself. Others are just witnesses of me following my thoughts, as I'm simply a witness to them following theirs.

– 96 –

Experiencing Concepts

My highest habit (or purpose) is to notice I have everything I need right now and then to experience it fully by leading from this context for life.

My Interpretations

_____

_____

_____

_____

_____

_____

_____

_____

_____

_____

_____

_____

_____

_____

_____

– 97 –

Unleashing Concepts

The closest I can get to predicting what I or another will do next is by observing my concepts and unleashing the anxious ones.

– 98 –

Motivated by Anxious-Free Concepts

I'm no longer seeking "The Truth." I'm just seeking and leading through anxious-free experiences.

My Interpretations

_____

_____

_____

_____

_____

_____

_____

_____

_____

_____

_____

_____

_____

_____

_____

_____

_____

– 99 –

Losing and Gaining Concepts

There is nothing to lose or gain but a concept and that I don't even have control over.

– 100 –

Self-Fulfilling Concepts

Everything could be considered as a concept and therefore, self-fulfilled.

My Interpretations

_____

_____

_____

_____

_____

_____

_____

_____

_____

_____

_____

_____

_____

_____

_____

Paying Attention...

The lessons drawn from this book empower managers, families, teachers and community leaders to honor what is available instead of paying attention to what isn't. Leaders of all ages now have a tool to take back the responsibility and unleash their leadership potential for igniting change in their workplace, home and community.

Interpretations

Upon purchasing this book, interpretations will be accessible on the website at www.JessieUpp.com.

For further exploration of rhetoric and awareness in general, you are invited to inquire the following: *"What questions would I ask of this observation to learn more?"* Once you register on the website, your inquiries, interpretations and comments are more than welcomed.

Share your interpretations with the world.

In a way, you become a co-author of any book you read. Regardless of your age, if you have something to share about one or more of these observations, your inquisitive thoughts are welcomed.

Submit your stick figure, textual, video or audio interpretations at www.JessieUpp.com. Serious or humorous, your analysis of each observation is invited!

After interpretations are collected from readers and leaders everywhere, the next version of this book will include a complete set of 100 epigrams...

Jessie Upp, M.S.

Jessie Upp specializes in a self-based leadership approach using innovative systems thinking, pedagogy and learning technologies. Having earned a Masters Degree in Management from the Center for Creative Change at Antioch University and a B.A. in Communications from WWU, her experiences have taken her from producing multimedia education in the corporate office to training youth, parents and mental health practitioners through her business during the last 10 years.

Ms. Upp now speaks on the concept of **Leading Without Anxiety**, which is applied in all observations found in this book. Through metaphorical and guided observations, she shares how leaders can drop the leash of control and create unique informed opportunities in their workplace, home and community.

Jessie lives in Edmonds, WA with her family and she continues to invite others to share their insights on leadership, from the family home to the corporate workplace.

As situations call, her dog (**Happy**) occasionally remains leashed.

www.ingramcontent.com/pod-product-compliance
Lightning Source LLC
Chambersburg PA
CBHW031948190326
41519CB00007B/720